Cow | Deer

Katie Mitchell, Nina Segal and Melanie Wilson

CW01497187

methuen | drama

LONDON • NEW YORK • OXFORD • NEW DELHI • SYDNEY

METHUEN DRAMA

Bloomsbury Publishing Plc, 50 Bedford Square, London, WC1B 3DP, UK
Bloomsbury Publishing Inc, 1359 Broadway, New York, NY 10018, USA
Bloomsbury Publishing Ireland, 29 Earlsfort Terrace, Dublin 2,
D02 AY28, Ireland

BLOOMSBURY, METHUEN DRAMA and the Methuen
Drama logo are trademarks of Bloomsbury Publishing Plc.

First published in Great Britain 2025

Cover image and design by Guy J Sanders

Bloomsbury Publishing Plc does not have any control over, or responsibility for,
any third-party websites referred to or in this book. All internet addresses given
in this book were correct at the time of going to press. The author and publisher
regret any inconvenience caused if addresses have changed or sites have ceased
to exist, but can accept no responsibility for any such changes.

No rights in incidental music or songs contained in the work are hereby
granted and performance rights for any performance/presentation
whatsoever must be obtained from the respective copyright owners.

All rights whatsoever in this play are strictly reserved and application
for performance etc. should be made before rehearsals begin to
The Agency, 170 Finchley Road, London, NW3 6BP, Curtis Brown Group,
28–29 Haymarket, London SW1Y 4SP and TEAM at hello@team-artists.co.uk.
No performance may be given unless a licence has been obtained.

A catalogue record for this book is available from the British Library.

Library of Congress Control Number: 2025944492

ISBN: PB: 978-1-3506-0240-3
ePDF: 978-1-3506-0241-0
eBook: 978-1-3506-0242-7

Series: Modern Plays

Typeset by Mark Heslington Ltd, Scarborough, North Yorkshire
Printed and bound in Great Britain

For product safety related questions contact
productsafety@bloomsbury.com.

To find out more about our authors and books visit
www.bloomsbury.com and sign up for our newsletters.

THE ROYAL COURT THEATRE AND
THE NATIONAL THEATRE OF GREECE
PRESENT

Cow | Deer

Co-created by Katie Mitchell, Nina Segal and Melanie Wilson

Cow | Deer was first performed at the Royal Court's Jerwood
Theatre Upstairs on Thursday 4 September 2025.

Cow | Deer
Co-created by Katie Mitchell, Nina Segal and Melanie Wilson

Cast (in alphabetical order)

Pandora Colin
Tom Espiner
Tatenda Matsvai
Ruth Sullivan

Co-Creator **Katie Mitchell**
Co-Creator **Nina Segal**
Co-Creator and Sound Artist **Melanie Wilson**
Designer **Alex Eales**
Lighting Designer **Prema Mehta**
Foley score originated by **Tom Espiner & Ruth Sullivan**
Associate Sound Designer & Operator **Marie Zschommler**
Casting Director **Saffeya Shebli**
Production Manager **Marius Rønning**
Assistant Production Manager **Tiffany Ledesma**
Costume Supervisor **Karen Hopkinson**
Company Manager **Mica Taylor**
Stage Manager **Louise Quartermain**
Deputy Stage Manager **Lucy Bradford**
Deputy Stage Manager Cover **Aimee Woods**
Lighting Supervisor **Izzy Hobby**
Lighting Programmer **Lizzie Skellett**
Lead Producer **Charlie Bunker for Impossible Producing**
Executive Producer **Steven Atkinson**

Initial development supported by the University of Oxford.

The Royal Court wish to thank the following for their help with this production:
Peter and Barbara Cozens, Trellyffaint Farm.

Katie Mitchell (Co-Creator)

Katie has directed over 100 productions in a career spanning forty years. She has been an Associate Director at the RSC, National Theatre and The Royal Court Theatre. She is currently Resident Director at the Berlin Schaubühne and the Hamburg Schaupielhaus. In 2009 she was awarded an OBE and in 2017 the British Academy's Presidents Medal for services to drama. She teaches extensively in universities, conservatoires and schools and is Professor of Theatre Directing at Royal Holloway University.

For the Royal Court: **Bluets, Anatomy of a Suicide, Ophelias Zimmer (& Berlin Schaubühne), 2071, Ten Billion, The City, The Country, Forty Winks, Nightsongs, Mountain Language/Ashes to Ashes, Live like Pigs.**

Other theatre includes: **Bernarda Albas Haus, 4.48 Psychosis, Travelling on One Leg, Happy Days** (Hamburg Schauspielhaus); **Orlando, Miss Julie, Lungs, The Yellow Wallpaper, Not the End of the World** (Schaubühne, Berlin); **The Maids** (Toneelgroep, Amsterdam); **A Sorrow Beyond Dreams** (Vienna Burgtheater); **Night Train, Rings of Saturn, Request Programme** (Cologne Schauspielhaus); **Easter, Krapps Last Tape, Night and Dreams** (Dramaten Theatre, Stockholm); **Cleansed, Women of Troy, Iphigenia at Aulis, Three Sisters, Ivanov, Dream Play, The Seagull, Waves, Dream Play** (National); **The Cherry Orchard, Ivanov** (Young Vic); **Little Scratch, Say it with Flowers, The Trial of Ubu** (Hampstead).

Opera includes: **Houses Slide** (Britten Sinfonia); **Pelleas et Melisande, Alcina, Trauernacht, The House Taken Over, Written on Skin** (Aix en Provence Festival); **The Blue Woman, Lucia di Lammermoor, Lessons in Love and Violence, Theodora** (Royal Opera House); **Le Vin Herbe, Neither** (Staatsoper, Berlin); **Al Gran Sole Carico D'Amore** (Salzburg Festival); **Orest, Jenufa** (Dutch National Opera); **St Matthew's Passion** (Glyndebourne Opera); **Bluebeard's Castle** (Munich Staatsoper).

Awards include: **Best Director for International Opera Awards, Golden Mask Award for Best Opera Director, The Tonic Award, The Stanislavsky International Prize, Best Director Nestroy Prize (Austria), Best Production Reumert Prize (Denmark), Golden Mask Award for Best Foreign Production (Russia), Europe Theatre Prize, OBIE Best Production Award, Evening Standard Best Director Award and the Theatertreffen Prize in 2008, 2009, 2020 and 2025.**

Nina Segal (Co-Creator)

For the Royal Court: **Dismantle This Room.**

Other theatre includes: **Shooting Hedda Gabler** (Rose); **The Good Person of Szechwan** (Sheffield Crucible/Lyric Hammersmith); **O, Island!** (RSC); **AI** (Young Vic); **Dismantle This Room** (Bush); **Big Guns** (Yard); **In the Night Time (Before the Sun Rises)** (Gate).

Opera includes: **We Are the Lucky Ones** (Dutch National Opera).

Melanie Wilson
(Co-Creator and Sound Artist)

For the Royal Court: **Anatomy of a Suicide, all of it.**

Other theatre includes: **Oracle Song (Barbican); Dreaming Species (online); Bernada Alba's Haus (Deutsches Schauspielhaus, Hamburg); Little Scratch (Hampstead & New Diorama); THEY (MIF); Unsere Zeit, (Residenztheater, Munich); Orlando (Schaubuehne, Berlin); When We Have Sufficiently Tortured Each Other, Cleansed (National); The Shape of the Pain (BAC); Kingdom Come (RSC); Landscape II (Dublin Festival); Reisende auf einem Bein (Deusches Schauspielhaus, Hamburg); The Forbidden Zone (Salzburg Festival/ International tour/Barbican); A Sorrow Beyond Dreams (Burgtheater, Vienna); Die Gelbe Tapete (Schaubuehne, Berlin); Reise Durch Die Nacht (Schauspeilhaus, Cologne); Autobiographer (Toynbee Studios/UK tour); Iris Brunette (Dublin Fringe).**

Opera includes: **glass human, (Glyndebourne), Current, Rising (ROH), Opera for the Unknown Woman (Wales Millenium Centre/Yorkshire International Festival).**

Television includes: **Where I Go (When I Can't Be Where I Am).**

Film includes: **No Light & No Land Anywhere.**

Awards includes: **Off West End Award for Best Sound Design (Autobiographer). Dublin Festival Award for Best Production (Iris Brunette).**

Lucy Bradford
(Deputy Stage Manager)

Theatre includes: **My Master Builder (Wyndham's); Jesus Christ Superstar (UK tour); Backstairs Billy (Duke of York's); Mamma Mia! (International tour); Orlando (Garrick); The Time Traveller's Wife (Chester Storyhouse); The Great British Bake Off Musical (Cheltenham Everyman); Beautiful: The Carole King Musical (UK tour); The Lemon Table (UK tour); Captain Corelli's Mandolin (Harold Pinter / UK tour); Decades, The Wizard of Oz, Random, Partition, Europe, Still Alice, The Fall of The Master Builder, Strictly Ballroom (Leeds Playhouse); Beyond These Walls (Northern Broadsides); The Chalk Garden (Chichester); Fidelio (Longborough Festival Opera); Spring and Port Wine (Oldham Collseum); Punkplay (Southwark); The Quiet House (Park / Birmingham Rep); Around the World in 80 Days (St James Theatre).**

Pandora Colin (Performer)

Theatre includes: **Abigail's Party (Stratford East); Dear Octopus, After The Dance, Every Good Boy Deserves Favour, Some Trace of Her, Women of Troy (National); Antigone, Our Town (Regent's Park); Bach and Sons (Bridge); No Particular Order, Top Trumps, Natural Selection (Theatre 503); 8 Hotels (Minerva, Chichester); A Midsummer Night's Dream, Julius Caesar, The Country Wife (Sheffield Crucible); Beginners (Unicorn); The Vote (Donmar); Cornelius – Brits off Broadway (59E59 Theatre, New York); The Dark Earth & The Light Sky, House Of Bernada Alba (Almeida); Sixty-Six Books, If There Is I Haven't Found It Yet (Bush): Stephen & The Sexy Partridge (Old Red Lion/Trafalgar Studios); Serious Money (Birmingham Repertory Theatre); Kindertransport, The Kiss (Hampstead); You Might As Well Live (New End Theatre/ Pleasance, Edinburgh); Mariana Pineda (Arcola); Much Ado About Nothing (Salisbury Playhouse); Design For Living, Fight for Barbara (Theatre Royal Bath); Man of Mode (Northcott Theatre Exeter); Buddy's Song (New Victoria Theatre).**

Television includes: **Eric, The Diplomat, Andor, Flatshare, Tom Jones, Master of None, Chernobyl, Delicious, Line of Duty, Count Arthur Strong, Penny Dreadful, Toast of London, Mr Selfridge, Doctors, Titanic, Hotel Babylon, Life Begins, Coupling, NY-LON, Black Books, Watermelon, Comedy Lab: The Pooters, The Dark Room, Extremely Dangerous, Close Relations, The Peter Principle, Wycliffe, Casualty, In Your Dreams, The Bill, Tears Before Bedtime.**

Film includes: **Earwig And The Witch, Aftermath, Film Stars Don't Die In Liverpool, The Lady In The Van, I Give It A Year, A Bunch Of Amateurs, Run, Fat Boy, Run, Max, What Rat's Won't Do.**

Radio includes: **Mueller: Trump Tower Moscow, Words and Music – Gratitude, The Amateur Marriage, With Great Pleasure, The Art of Deception – Women's Hour, Book at Bedtime – Summer Crossing, The Happiness Foundation.**

Pandora also performs cabaret as drag king, Ray Jissues (say it all together).

Alex Eales (Designer)

For the Royal Court: **Bluets, Not I/Footfalls/ Rockaby (& West End), Anatomy of a Suicide.**

Other theatre includes: **The Pillowman (Gate, Dublin); Portia Coughlan (Almeida); Grapes of Wrath, Cleansed (National); Limehouse (Donmar); East is South, Say It With Flowers and small hours (Hampstead); Hamlet (Bristol Old Vic); Oleanna (Theatre Royal Bath and West End); Norma Jeane Baker of Troy (The Shed, New York); Fraulein Julie, Orlando and Schatten - Eurydike sagt (Schaubühne, Berlin); Bernarda Albas Haus, Der Kirschgarten, Bluets, Schlafende Männer, 4.48 Psychose, Reisende auf einem Bein and Alles weitere kennen Sie aus dem Kino (Deutsches Schauspielhaus, Hamburg); Maladie de la Mort (Bouffes du Nord, Paris and European tour); Regeneration (Royal, Northampton); Into the Woods (Théâtre du Châtelet, Paris); Reise durch die Nacht (Schauspielhaus, Cologne, Berlin and Avignon festival); The Breath Of Life (Lyceum Theatre, Sheffield); Wunschkonzert (Schauspielhaus, Cologne and Berlin); Jungfruleken (Kungsliga Dramatiska Teatern, Stockholm).**

Opera includes: **William Tell (Opera de Lausanne); La Voix Humaine (Opera du**

Rhin); Un ballo in Maschera (Royal Danish Opera and Norwegian National Opera); Il trovatore (Hamburg Staatsoper); Judith - Concerto For Orchestra / Bluebeard's Castle (Bayerisches Staatsoper, Munich); Rigoletto and Macbeth (Opera Theatre of St Louis); Falstaff (Shanghai Opera House); Le nozze di Figaro (Salzburg Festival); The House Taken Over (Festival d'Aix-en-Provence); Cosi fan Tutte (Opera Holland Park); Clemency (ROH2 Linbury Studio and Scottish Opera); Idomeneo (English National Opera); Tarantula in Petrol Blue (Aldeburgh Music). Designs for Dance include: Cri de Coeur (Paris Opera Ballet, Opéra Palais Garnier); Bon Voyage, Bob (Tanztheater Wuppertal Pina Bausch, Germany).

Tom Espiner (Performer)

Theatre includes: **Boys On The Verge Of Tears (Soho Theatre); Witness For The Prosecution (County Hall), Life of Pi (Sheffield Crucible/ West End); Berberian Sound Studio (Donmar); Macbeth, Twelfth Night, The Winter's Tale (Shakespeare at the Tobacco Factory); Anything Goes, Love's Labour's Lost (National); The Firework Maker's Daughter (Told by an Idiot/Lyric Hammersmith); Peggy for You (Hampstead/West End); Tombstone Tales (Arcola); The Magic Flute (Complicite/ Dutch National Opera); Caucasian Chalk Circle, Britain's Best Recruiting Sergeant (Unicorn); An Oak Tree (Traverse); Ether Frolics (Sound&Fury with artists from Shunt); Kursk (Sound&Fury/Young Vic/ Sydney Opera House); Going Dark (London Science Museum/Sound&Fury).**

Television includes: **Industry, Chloe, The Crown, Ancient Rome: The Rise and Fall of an Empire, Without Motive, Casualty, The Bill.**

Film includes: **Anybody's Nightmare, Stoned.**

Foley design and consulting includes: **Berberian Sound Studio, When Winston Went To War With The Wireless (Donmar); The Walrus Has a Right To Adventure (Liverpool Everyman); The Fir Tree (How it Ended/Arts Depot); The Magic Flute (Complicite/DNO 2012); The Boy Who Always Looked Up (Ryan Gander/2 Willow Road).**

Foley for film & television includes: **Numerous Natural History films, Stagefright, Rex the Runt, King Rollo Films, Dirty Bomb, Lawless.**

As co-creator and performer, for Sound&Fury Theatre Company: **War Music, The Watery Part of the World, Ether Frolics, Kursk, Going Dark, Charlie Ward.**

Puppetry with Blind Summit includes: **The Table (Spoleto festival USA and European tour); The Puppeteer (Lorca Institute, Granada, Spain/ Il Funaro/ Pleasance); Madam Butterfly (ENO); Danny Boyle's London 2012 Olympics Opening Ceremony.**

Puppetry direction includes: **Great Apes (Arcola); Meet Fred (Hijinx).**

Tiffany Ledesma
(Assistant Production Manager)

Theatre includes: **Everything Has Disappeared (Mammalian Diving Reflex/ international tour); The Fixing Girl, Truth, It's A Wonderful Life, Snow White, Bent Boy (Young People's Theatre, Toronto); Three Ordinary Men (Cahoots, Toronto); Our Fathers, Sons, Lovers, and Little Brothers (Tarragon, Toronto/tour).**

Tatenda Matsvai (Performer)

Theatre includes: **Dark Matter, Hot in Here (Gate); Hot Orange (Halfmoon Theatre).**

Awards include: **VAULT Festival Origin Award for Outstanding New Work (Dark Matter).**

Prema Mehta (Lighting Designer)

For the Royal Court: **Superhoe.**

Other theatre includes: **A Day in the Death of Joe Egg (West End); Bartholomew Fair, Richard II (Globe); Studio Créole (Manchester International Festival); Things of Dry Hours (Young Vic); The Hired Man (& Queen's, Hornchurch/Hull Truck), The Importance of Being Earnest (Octagon, Bolton); Of Kith & Kin (& Bush), Chicken Soup (Crucible, Sheffield); Fame (Selladoor/UK tour/Peacock); East is East (& Northern Stage), Holes, Hercules (Nottingham Playhouse); Talking Heads (Leeds Playhouse); A Midsummer Night's Dream (Curve, Leicester); Mighty Atoms (Hull Truck); A Passage to India (Royal & Derngate, Northampton/UK tour); The Wizard of Oz (Storyhouse); The York Suffragettes, Murder, Margaret & Me (Theatre Royal, York); Love Lies & Taxidermy, Growth, I Got Superpowers for**
My Birthday (Paines Plough); Coming Up, Jefferson's Garden, Fourteen (Watford Palace); The Electric Hills (Liverpool Everyman); The Great Extension (Theatre Royal, Stratford East); The Snow Queen (Derby Theatre); Huddle (Unicorn); Wipers (UK tour).**

Dance includes: **Bells (Mayor of London Presents: Showtime Festival); Spill (Düsseldorf); Sufi Zen (Royal Festival Hall); Dhamaka (O2 Arena); Maaya (Westminster Hall).**

Live events include: **A-List Party Area (Madame Tussauds).**

Louise Quartermain
(Stage Manager)

Theatre includes: **My Master Builder (Wyndham's); Jesus Christ Superstar (UK tour); Backstairs Billy (Duke of York's); Mamma Mia! (International tour); Orlando (Garrick); The Time Traveller's Wife (Chester Storyhouse); The Great British Bake Off Musical (Cheltenham Everyman); Beautiful: The Carole King Musical (UK tour); The Lemon Table (UK tour); Captain Corelli's Mandolin (Harold Pinter / UK tour); Decades, The Wizard of Oz, Random, Partition, Europe, Still Alice, The Fall of The Master Builder, Strictly Ballroom (Leeds Playhouse); Beyond These Walls (Northern Broadsides); The Chalk Garden (Chichester); Fidelio (Longborough Festival Opera); Spring and Port Wine (Oldham Coliseum); Punkplay (Southwark); The Quiet House (Park / Birmingham Rep); Around the World in 80 Days (St James Theatre).**

Ruth Sullivan (Performer)

Theatre includes: **Twelfth Night, Kingdom, The Norman Conquests, Happy Days (Tower); 1984, Nancy (Theatro Technis); Evelyn – Kindertransport (Theatro Technis / Gatehouse).**

As foley artist, television includes: **The Lawyer (Shardlake), Top Boy, The Lazarus Project, The Long Shadow, The Great, The Gold, Inside No. 9, The Capture, Peaky Blinders, Silent Witness, Feel Good, Bodyguard, Killing Eve, The Durrells, Jamestown, Black Mirror, Poldark, Fearless, Rillington Place, Dickensian, Downton Abbey, The Musketeers, The Casual Vacancy, Any Human Heart.**

As foley artist, film includes: **My Sister's Bones, The Critic, The Full Monty 23, The Wonder, Scrapper, Hamlet, Above the Clouds, Peterloo, Ophelia, Dead in a Week (Or Your Money Back), The Death of Stalin, Golden Years, Desert Dancer, 28 Days Later, Creation, The Boat that Rocked, Mamma Mia!, The World is Not Enough, Eyes Wide Shut, Running Free, Proof, The Life and Death of Peter Sellers, My House in Umbria, The Hours, In America, The Four Feathers, Enigma, Still Crazy, Twin Town.**

Live foley artist for theatre includes: **Die Zauberflöte/The Magic Flute (Dutch National Opera, Amsterdam/ ENO London/ The Metropolitan Opera, New York/ Aix-en-Provence Festival/ Bergen National Opera/ Palau de Sophia, Valencia); Storm Exercise; dir. Janina Lange (Turf Projects, Croydon); To Hull and Back (Hull City Hall); Lea e il Gomitolo (Royal College of Art, London); Wunschloses Unglück (A Sorrow Beyond Dreams) (Burgteater, Vienna); Cabaret (Royal Danish Theatre, Copenhagen); The Hush (The Shed/ National); The Rings of Saturn (Die Ringe des Saturn) (Halle Kirk, Schauspiel Cologne & Gymnase du lycée Aubanel, Avignon Festival).**

As foley consultant, theatre includes: **Die Zauberflöte (Basal Opera); Brief Encounter, Spike (Watermill Theatre/National tour); Sensory Stories: Journey to the Cornfield (National Gallery art project for Tyne and Wear Museums); Edmond de Bergerac (Birmingham Repertory Theatre); The Yellow Wallpaper (Die gelbe Tapete) (Schaubühne, Berlin); A Midsummer Night's Dream (Storyhouse, Chester).**

As director, theatre includes: **The Worst Witch, hang (Tower Theatre); Bouncers and Shakers, Air, Charles III (Tower Theatre); Air Tower Theatre as part of the Love [and Survival] in a Time of Covid festival); Rosencrantz and Guildenstern are Dead (Gatehouse); The Maids, The Mystery of Edwin Drood (Theatro Technis); Macbeth (Shoreditch Church/Jardin Shakespeare, Paris); The Last Five Years (Courtyard Theatre); The Sea (Bridewell Theatre).**

As sound designer, theatre includes: **A Dream Play, Leave Taking, Bouncers and Shakers, Tituba, Mules, King Charles III (Tower Theatre); A Westminster Story (Waterloo East); The Net (Tristan Bates Theatre); The Winter's Tale (Bridewell Theatre & Jardin Shakespeare, Paris); Di and Viv and Rose, Frozen (Theatro Technis); The Ladykillers by Graham Linehan, One Man, Two Guv'nors, Time and the Conways (Gatehouse); Might Never Happen (King's Head Theatre & UK Schools tour); The Accrington, Gomenghast (Bridewell Theatre).**

Awards include: **Emmy Award for Outstanding Sound Editing for a Miniseries, Movie or a Special (The Life and Death of Peter Sellers), Verna Fields Award (The Pride of Wade Ellison).**

Aimee Woods
(Deputy Stage Manager Cover)

For the Royal Court: **ECHO.**

Other theatre Includes: **Fat Ham, The Provoked Wife, Timon of Athens and Tamburlaine (RSC), Passing Strange, Beneatha's Place and The Second Woman (Young Vic), The Odyssey (National) I Should Be So Lucky (UK tour), Strictly Ballroom (UK tour), Phantom of the Opera (West End).**

Marie Zschommler (Associate Sound Designer & Operator)

As sound designer, theatre includes: **Barriers (UK tour); Earthquakes in London, A Dream (Royal and Derngate); Grusome Playground Injuries (The Glitch); The Promise (UK tour); The Vagina Monologues (Hackney Empire/UK tour); Funeral Sandwiches (Drayton Arms).**

As associate sound designer, theatre includes: **Anne Boleyn The Musical (Hever Castle); Ben And Imo (RSC, Orange Tree); Abigails Party (Royal Exchange); Bernada Albas Haus (SchauSpielHaus Hamburg); RUCKUS (UK tour); Walking Cats (Vaults festival); The Trials Of Josie K (Stratford Youth Zone, Unicorn); A Christmas Carole (Southend Palace).**

THE ROYAL COURT THEATRE

The Royal Court Theatre is the writers' theatre. It is a leading force in world theatre for cultivating and supporting writers - undiscovered, emerging and established.

Since 1956, we have commissioned and produced hundreds of writers, from John Osborne to Joel Tan. Royal Court plays from every decade are now performed on stages and taught in classrooms and universities across the globe.

Through the writers, the Royal Court is at the forefront of creating restless, alert, provocative theatre about now. We open our doors to the unheard voices and free thinkers that, through their writing, change our way of seeing.

We strive to create an environment in which differing voices and opinions can co-exist. In current times, it is becoming increasingly difficult for writers to write what they want or need to write without fear, and we will do everything we can to rise above a narrowing of viewpoints. Through all our work, we strive to inspire audiences and influence future writers with radical thinking and provocative discussion.

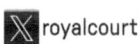 royalcourt  royalcourttheatre

NATIONAL THEATRE OF GREECE

The National Theatre, centered in Athens, Greece, has in its mission to promote theatre and culture, nurture creativity, and connect theatre with communities both locally and internationally. Under the new artistic direction of Argyro Chioti and Deputy Io Voulgaraki, the National Theatre of Greece is becoming a vibrant space where tradition meets innovation, local stories connect with global voices, and fresh perspectives come to life.

While continuing to support and evolve its core missions, which include developing and staging Greek dramaturgy, modern, classic and ancient drama, research, exploration and experimentation in new forms of theatre and modes of stage expression as well as producing theatre for young people and children and providing theatre education, the focus is even more now on outward engagement and dynamic exchange.

Founded in 1901 as the Royal Theatre and designed by Ernst Ziller, the National Theatre reopened in 1930 and has since grown steadily, with a permanent troupe and a continuously operating Drama School. Becoming a non-profit in 1994, it preserves Greek cultural identity through diverse productions and fosters international collaborations. Today, it operates six stages across its historic venues. Since 2022, is a proud member of the European Theatre Convention, Europe's largest theatre network and develops artistic residencies programs, showcases, workshops and innovative European programs related to critical social matters of the world.

ROYAL COURT SUPPORTERS

Our incredible community of supporters makes it possible for us to achieve our mission of nurturing and platforming writers at every stage of their careers. Our supporters are part of our essential fabric – they help to give us the freedom to take bigger and bolder risks in our work, develop and empower new voices, and create world-class theatre that challenges and disrupts the theatre ecology.

To all our supporters, thank you. You help us to write the future.

PUBLIC FUNDING

CORPORATE SPONSORS & SUPPORTERS
Aqua Financial Ltd
Cadogan
Character 7
Concord Theatricals
Edwardian Hotels, London
NJA Ltd. – Core Values & Creative Management
Nick Hern Books
Phone Locker
Riverstone Living
Sustainable Wine Solutions
Walpole

CORPORATE MEMBERS
Bloomberg Philanthopies
Sloane Stanley

TRUSTS & FOUNDATIONS

Backstage Trust
Bruce Wake Charitable Trust
Chalk Cliff Trust
Clare McIntyre's Bursary
Cockayne - Grants for the Arts
The Common Humanity Arts Trust
Cowley Charitable Foundation
David Laing Foundation
The Davidson PlayGC Bursary
The Fenton Arts Trust
Foyle Foundation
Genesis Foundation
The Golsoncott Foundation
Jerwood Foundation
John Thaw Foundation
The Katie Bradford Arts Trust
The Lynne Gagliano Writers' Award
The Marlow Trust
Martin Bowley Charitable Trust
Molecule Theatre Ltd
The Noël Coward Foundation
Old Possum's Practical Trust
Richard Radcliffe Charitable Trust
The Royal Borough of Kensington & Chelsea Arts Grant
Rose Foundation
The Thistle Trust
The Thompson Family Charitable Trust
The T.S. Eliot Foundation
Unity Theatre Trust
Y.A.C.K F.O

INDIVIDUAL SUPPORTERS

Artistic Director's Circle

Eric Abraham
Katie Bradford
Jeremy & Becky Broome
Clyde Cooper
Debbie De Girolamo &
Ben Babcock
Dominique & Neal Gandhi
Lydia & Manfred Gorvy
David & Jean Grier
Charles Holloway OBE
Linda Keenan
Andrew Rodger and Ariana
Neumann
Jack Thorne & Rachel Mason
Sandra Treagus for
ATA Assoc. LTD
Sally Whitehill & Mark Gordon
Anonymous

Writers' Circle

Chris & Alison Cabot
Cas Donald
Robyn Durie
The Hon P N Gibson's Charity
Trust
Kater Gordon
Ellie & Roger Guy
Melanie J. Johnson
Nicola Kerr
Héloïse and Duncan
Matthews KC
Emma O'Donoghue
Clare Parsons & Tony Langham
Maureen & Tony Wheeler
Anonymous

Directors' Circle

Piers Butler
Fiona Clements
Professor John Collinge
Julian & Ana Garel-Jones
Carol Hall
Dr Timothy Hyde
Elizabeth O'Connor & Adam
Bandeen

Platinum Circle

Moira Andreae
Beverley Buckingham
Katie Bullivant
Anthony Burton CBE
Matthew Dean
Lucy & Spencer De Grey
Emily Fletcher
The Edwin Fox Foundation
Beverley Gee
Madeleine Hodgkin
Kate Howe
Roderick & Elizabeth Jack
Susanne Kapoor
David P Kaskel & Christopher
A Teano
Peter & Maria Kellner
Frances Lynn
Robert Ledger & Sally
Moulsdale
Mrs Janet Martin
Andrew McIver
Barbara Minto
Brian and Meredith Niles
Timothy Prager
Corinne Rooney
Sir Paul & Lady Ruddock
Sir William & Lady Russell
Anita Scott
Bhags Sharma
Dr Wendy Sigle
Rita Skinner
James and Victoria Tanner
Mrs Caroline Thomas
Yannis Vasatis
Ian, Victoria and Lucinda
Watson
Sir Robert & Lady Wilson

With thanks to our Silver and
Gold Supporters, and our
Friends and Good Friends,
whose support we greatly
appreciate.

Let's be friends. With benefits.

Our Friends and Good Friends are part of the fabric of the Royal Court. They help us to create world-class theatre, and in return they receive early access to our shows and a range of exclusive benefits.

Join today and become a part of our community.

Become a Friend (from £40 a year)

Benefits include:

- Priority Booking
- Advanced access to £15 Monday tickets
- 10% Bar & Kitchen discount (including Court in the Square)

Become a Good Friend (from £95 a year)

In addition to the Friend benefits, our Good Friends also receive:

- Five complimentary playtexts for Royal Court productions
- An invitation for two to step behind the scenes of the Royal Court Theatre at a special event

Our Good Friends' membership also includes a voluntary donation. This extra support goes directly towards supporting our work and future, both on and off stage.

To become a Friend or a Good Friend, or to find out more about the different ways in which you can get involved, visit our website: royalcourttheatre.com/support-us

The English Stage Company at the Royal Court Theatre is a registered charity (No. 231242)

Cow | Deer and the Climate Emergency

Why is the climate emergency largely absent from contemporary theatre? Is it through lack of awareness? Necessary denial? Understandable fear? Or because the specifics of the climate emergency - the scale of it, the span of it, the existential threat of it - are particularly difficult to stage?

The climate emergency is a subject that resists the forms of storytelling we are most used to. There is no neat beginning or tidy ending; nor clear protagonists or single heroes - we are all implicated in this story, both as protagonist and antagonist. Neither can the subject be contained within a single narrative, nor discrete place - this crisis has a global setting, spanning continents and countries (even as the brunt of its effects are disproportionately falling on the Global South). It is a story with a new and variable cast of characters - the sea, the air, the glaciers - as well as all the living creatures in the more-than-human world, so rarely represented on stage. The climate emergency is a defining crisis of our time - the threat of it is existential. If existing storytelling mechanisms cannot tell this story, then we must explore new tools.

Cow | Deer is an attempt to look beyond the human stories of the climate crisis, towards the more-than-human world; to use a set of tools outside of human language (being a performance without spoken word) to offer audiences another narrative, that of the more-than-human world - the animals, the insects, the environment itself. The climate crisis is, in part, a failure to acknowledge and to understand this natural world as more than just a backdrop for our human narratives - we are not the only characters in this story. Instead, we are part of a fragile and complex environment; and our existence must be in collaboration - thoughtful, careful, equitable collaboration - with the natural world. *Cow | Deer* is an experiment, in which we make an offer of a deeper kind of connection; the kind of deep and equitable attention that might enable us to navigate this crisis, in collaboration with each other and the more-than-human world.

*

From the colonies of microbes in our guts and the plants with whom we breathe, to the industrialised uteruses who feed us, other beings compose us. Making space for them within our culture is a defining challenge for viable human futures. Listening, a traditionally under explored act within performance-making, offers a way of thinking differently into this space.

Listening to the world is a process of stilling oneself, of tuning into what exists. This tuning in includes an awareness of our position as a listener in relation to the places and beings being listened to, or listened with. There is no objective point from which to listen, we are always listening from within a set of relationships with the world that sounds around us.

This can be thought of as feminist listening. A kind of listening that turns towards the sounds and voices that cannot be heard or are yet to be revealed, the submerged or the speculative. When we make space to listen together in this way, we make space for new stories about time, intelligence, kinship and the web of life we are held in. This rebalancing is urgent, empathetic work, for we must find our way through to a better accommodation between ourselves and the other species if we are all to survive. We have an opportunity to listen, deeply, for ourselves as stewards, not extractors of life.

Katie Mitchell, Nina Segal and Melanie Wilson

Foley and Performance

Foley is the technique of performing and recording sound effects that synchronise with a moving image. It is a craft that originated in filmmaking, and forms one of the key sonic elements for soundtrack creation in moving image, television, documentary, animation, computer games and radio (where it's known as spot effects).

The technique emerged in the late 1920s in the early days of film, developed by stuntman Jack Foley, for whom the art form is named. Initially, Foley would join the recording sessions of the orchestral score, performing certain sounds to match the stunts seen on screen. From those beginnings, he developed the technique into a more detailed strand, moving into his own room, 'Foley's Room', which in turn became the Foley studio familiar with moving image makers and Foley artists today. More people joined him to provide extra footsteps and other sounds, and became known as the Foley Walkers.

Foley artists recreate the sound of everything that moves on screen, as it's not possible to capture these sounds during the noise of the filming process. These sounds can include walking, running, chewing, pouring tea, creaking chairs, fighting, gun effects and machine and body impacts. Foley artists create the sounds the actors make and other non-organic sounds too, such as thunder, wind and the movement of gravel beneath a tyre as a car speeds past.

These sounds help the viewer to focus on the action of the scene, and support details of the script or the actor's performance. For example, picking out the sound of the clothing conveys information on the wealth and status of the character and the specific period setting of the drama. Foley sound also underpins the emotional state of the character - the nervous jangling of keys, the frantic shuffling of papers, the precision of lighting a cigar all add to the drama of the scene. The Foley artist interprets and supports the intensity of performance as a form of performance itself.

Alongside the creation of sound effects, the Foley art form also includes the amplification and treatment of the sounds created, and their placement within the wider sound world.

More recently, the Foley technique has begun to move beyond film and moving image, to feature in theatre and opera. This move has an echo of the past, when music hall performers would perform live sound to accompany action. Foley's contemporary evolution into live performance blends the technicality of its filmmaking lineage with an innate theatrical appeal as a highly skilled performance language.

Katie Mitchell's use of Foley techniques in live performance began with her Live Cinema production of *Wunchkonzert* at Cologne Schauspielhaus, in 2008. Live

Cinema is a form which combines theatre with filmmaking techniques, using Foley to focus the audience's attention on a particular detail or perspective within the work. Katie Mitchell and Melanie Wilson began working together in 2013, using live Foley in Live Cinema productions to centralise the experience of the central female character, by highlighting the tiny details of the movement of clothing or objects or actions like walking or swimming. Ruth Sullivan has worked with Katie and Melanie as advisor, trainer and performer of Foley techniques in Live Cinema productions since 2012, when she performed in *The Rings of Saturn* in Cologne. Katie and Melanie have also explored the use of Foley in productions that were not Live Cinema - notably in *little scratch* at Hampstead Theatre in 2021 and, for Katie, her production of *The Cherry Orchard* in 2022, using live Foley to animate the more-than-human world of trees, mammals and insects, and to centre the perspective of the trees. *Cow / Deer* builds on this shared body of work - drawing on Melanie, Katie and Ruth's use of Foley thus far, with a shared but independently explored focus on ecology and theatre-making.

*

For *Cow / Deer* Ruth Sullivan is joined by Tom Espiner as Foley artists and originators of the Foley score. Tom and Ruth's independent Foley work spans multiple contexts of Foley sound creation for moving image, nature documentary and live performance. For Tom and Ruth the use of Foley in *Cow / Deer* is unique - as it requires four performers and the sound operator to listen and collaborate as an ensemble, in relationship with the field recording score. Ruth describes this as 'orchestral', a form of sound-making that is as much music-making or acting as Foley. "Usually I am relying only on myself, but in this project we must learn how to create a sound picture as a team", Ruth says. Both Tom and Ruth see this live ensemble form as an interesting evolution in Foley, allowing them to create all elements of an animal's movements concurrently. In Foley, usually the footsteps, fur, breath, tail swish and udder movement of a cow would all be created and recorded separately, then layered to create a unified sound image. In *Cow / Deer*, these elements can be created simultaneously, through the ensemble listening and working together, accompanied by field recordings, to produce a live, real-time sonic rendition of the action.

Tom reflects on being released, in *Cow / Deer*, from the need to sync sound with image as entering "an imaginative realm, where the moving image takes place in our mind's eye. It's not a straightforward piece of music, it's a story. We are calibrating the signature rhythm of how each animal moves and ensuring the intensity and pace of that movement is appropriate to the events unfolding in the narrative. It sharpens the performers' powers of imagination; we have to be selective and restrained, waiting for our moment to contribute our element to the picture". This imaginative act is one the project hopes to instil in the audience too.

In conversation with Tom and Ruth, they both reflect on whether the term Foley is an accurate description for how the art form functions in theatre - being that its strict definition involves the creation of sound effects for recording, not for live performance. There is potential, Ruth thinks, for conceiving of their work as live sound performing, rather than Foley - especially, Tom thinks, since the term is increasingly used in theatre as a shorthand for aspects of sound or performance that are strictly beyond its scope.

In contemplating the effect of this choreographic form of Foley sound on the listener, Ruth says, "We need to work carefully to bring the audience with us, so that they 'see' what we're doing in each step and event". Tom adds, "I think the audience will go in and out of the imaginative world, sometimes they'll be in the natural world locations, sometimes in the theatre, listening and watching the performers create that world".

The relationship between the Foley, field recordings and sound design is a key part of understanding this imaginative world. Tom reflects that "Foley sound effects on their own don't work, they're only part of the picture. They need to be embedded within a multi-layered soundscape in order to make sense and to tell the story, sonically and emotionally".

Tom reflects on how Foley in nature documentary builds an important, if necessarily constructed, connection to the animals it features: "No microphone in the world will get close enough to a polar bear to capture the close-up perspective that long-range photography achieves - so we have to use Foley to imaginatively create that sense of intimate animal presence". *Cow / Deer* attempts to do the same - offering the audience a close-up listening experience through Foley that would not be possible in nature.

The interplay in *Cow / Deer* between Foley sound, ecological soundscapes and story offers the audience a way to listen differently - not only in the context of theatre and performance-making, but in relation to the way animals listen to us and the world. Research shows that certain species hear different parts of the frequency spectrum - some much higher or lower than human hearing. Knowing this, perhaps us humans can interrogate our own way of listening to the world - what do we hear and what do we fail to hear? And how can Foley and field recordings - and the depth of listening experience offered in *Cow / Deer* - encourage us to listen more closely to the more-than-human world?

Melanie Wilson

The Politics of Foley in Cow | Deer

Traditionally Foley has taken place in a sound-sealed booth, which creates a controlled environment in which to create high-quality audio. Indeed, this is the way that Melanie and Katie have previously used Foley in their Live Cinema collaborations. In these works, with the Foley taking place within a separate booth, the live Foley exists at a necessary remove from the visual action.

In *Cow | Deer* we have removed the link between the visual source and the sonic response - choosing instead to focus on Foley as a distinct and originating sonic art form in relationship with a text. We have also chosen not to seal the performers in a booth, separated from the audience, but to position them within the sound field, at the centre of the listening perspective of the animals that lead this piece. In conversation with the eco acoustic practice of field recording, and the lineage of Foley as it operates in nature documentary, we are creating a politics for this project which foregrounds the more-than-human world through listening.

The listening experience of *Cow | Deer* allows the visual world mapped in the text to unfold in the imagination of the audience, carried by the sound images created by the Foley and the field recordings. Yet there remains an innate visual performativity in the creation of Foley - full of the visual data of the materials, bodies, faces and hands of the Foley artists.

We are working with this unique form of performative listening labour to thread a theme of human stewardship for the more-than-human world through the project. This theme emerges from our aim to centralise the narratives of other beings, whilst also contending with the indelible influence our human actions have on those bodies. In this way Foley offers us a way to sink deeply into the imaginative possibilities of hearing the world with animal ears - whilst always calling us back to the fragility, tenderness and responsibility of our bond with these other life forms.

Melanie Wilson

Preparing the Text for Rehearsals

I normally prepare six layers of information when directing a play: place (the location of the scene), time (the year, season, day of the week and time of day the scene takes place in), character biography (a timeline of the character's life), immediate circumstances (the 24 hours before each scene starts), events (the changes in the scene affecting all the characters) and intentions (what the character wants the other character/s to do, say or feel). In rehearsals these six layers are refined by the performers and creative team. With *Cow | Deer* these six layers were applied - albeit cautiously because we were wary of anthropomorphising the animals.

A map of place was constructed, including the relationship between the farm buildings and the nursery field (where the pregnant cow is) and the field's relationship to the woodland and cornfield where the deer roams. The map was shaped by Nina's imagination, Melanie's field recordings and a research trip to Trellyffaint Farm in Pembrokeshire to see the layout of a real dairy farm. The finished map offers the performers a picture of where each animal is in each scene and where all the places (or other animals) are which they listen or respond to.

The play occurs in August 2025 and the time of day is described in each scene. We decided on Friday as the day because human beings are sometimes tired then and may not always keep a good eye on the road. Animals operate inside very different time frames to humans – a deer can be up all night and then asleep in the day, specifically between noon and 4pm. Cows sleep in short intervals throughout the day and night, totalling four hours of sleep in any 24-hour period. Time of day therefore has different impacts on animal behaviour compared to how it affects humans. The four layers of time (year, season, day of the week, time of day), help the performers articulate how time impacts the animals' experience.

When building a character biography for humans, we bring our own knowledge of human behaviour to the task. For example, when we notice a characteristic, we can invent an incident in that character's past to generate that behaviour. With animals the task can be the same - for example, the deer's fear of the electric fence can be supported by an incident in her biography where she was electrocuted by an electric fence. However, animals' brains are structured differently to humans' - although animals are sentient and do experience emotion, their behaviour is not generated in the same way. Deer, for example, have short-term and long-term memories but their memory systems are used primarily for survival, such as remembering food sources, water locations, travel routes and safe areas. These differences meant we had to unpick how we construct human psychology to allow for the more-than-human experience. Biographies offer the performers a shared picture of incidents in the animal's past which help them articulate the animal's present experience precisely.

Cow / Deer runs mostly in chronological order with few time jumps, so we only needed to build three immediate circumstance timelines, one before Scene 1, and two during the action. Imagining being active all night or only sleeping in snatches invited us into the new experience of the more-than-human world. These animal timelines, like human ones, support the performers in articulating the effect of the passage of time on the animals.

We discovered that events in this play were often linked to physical sensation, like the feeling of a fly on fur - but there were also clear emotions, like fear or loss, but not thoughts (as humans experience thinking). Pinpointing these physical and emotional changes in the action allows the performers to articulate precisely how changes affect the animals' experience in the action.

Intentions are designed around human internal processes, so it was initially challenging to apply them to animal experience. Yet cows and deer do have cognitive abilities, including learning, memory and problem-solving skills. Cows also live in social groups with complex relationships within the group as well as having relationships with human beings. This research allowed us to imagine the animals' intentions at any given moment - while avoiding projecting a human version of their desires onto them.

Applying these six layers (originally designed to clarify human characters) to animal characters invited us into the experience, processing, cognitive and emotional aspects of animal reality. This allowed us to understand more fully where human and animal experience coincides and diverges. There is scope here to repurpose the tools we use to present humans to portray the similarly complex experience of animals. Perhaps there is a future of theatre programming which strikes a better balance between staging stories about human beings with stories about the more-than-human world.

Katie Mitchell

Cow | Deer: A Performance for Sound

Cow | Deer is a performance for sound - utilising live Foley performance and a sound score of collected field recordings to invite the audience into the more-than-human world.

The performance has no words.

This text - a written document of the production - consists entirely of words.

Reading this text will inevitably be different to experiencing the piece as performed. And yet, that is the case for all playtexts - the written document is always at some distance from the live experience. What follows is an attempt to bridge that distance - to equip the reader to successfully conjure this wordless performance from the following pages of words.

Cow | Deer is performed by live Foley performers, accompanied by a sound score of collected field recordings. These performers - in the original production - were made up of two Foley artists and two actors trained in Foley, working with and on a range of surfaces and materials, arranged in front of the audience. The surfaces included: two tables supporting straw bales, a raised water tank, a strip of turf, a collection of metal sheets, some potted trees and plants and a small sound booth. The theatre space was designed to be a functional Foley studio - created to support the work of sound-making, rather than imposing a narrative upon it. The live Foley and the collected field recordings are amplified through a seventeen-channel sound system, placed around, above and below the audience.

These sound elements - the live Foley and the field recordings - can be thought of as in conversation with each other; and in conversation with the text that forms the 'story' or the 'action' of the piece. While the piece itself is wordless, this text forms a kind of skeleton - providing the internal structure that the sound world builds upon. Yet it is not as straightforward as the sound staging the story - the process of making this piece has been collaborative and iterative, with the capabilities and possibilities of sound exerting their own influence upon the text. There is a circularity - the sound world influencing the text, the propositions of the text influencing the sound world. This is reflected in the layout of this document - with the left column of text describing the 'action' and the right column of text describing the live Foley effects, field recordings and sound design that realise this action in performance.

This first column - being more similar to traditional stage directions or descriptions of action - requires less explanation. The second column may benefit from more - especially for those who did not experience *Cow | Deer* live.

- Where 'Foley' is referenced, this describes the materials used to create the specific events or sequences described in the 'action' column.

- Where 'Field recording' is referenced, this describes the pre-recorded material - composed, edited and mixed - that is heard alongside the live Foley, evoking the immediate environment described in the 'action' column.

- Where 'Sound design' is referenced, this describes the way sound is processed to give a sense of space or movement - for instance, as a car passes the field and then recedes. It also denotes which animal's perspective the audience experience the sound world from - listening from 'between the ears' of either COW or DEER.

- Some of the Foley cues take place in the booth onstage, which allows the sound to be controlled spatially. An example of this can be seen in scene four - as footsteps approach COW from a distance, walk around her, then move back across the field. In this moment, the live footsteps created by the Foley artist will fade in, be heard to circle round the audience and then recede - with the audience experiencing the movement of the farmer from the same perspective as COW.

Many of the objects used to create certain animals or ecological textures in this piece are widely used by contemporary Foley artists - but some have been specifically sourced and conceived by Tom Espiner and Ruth Sullivan, the originators of the piece's Foley score, as part of their unique practice of the form. Examples of this include a particular bladder used in horse surgery, utilised to create the sound of COW urinating, conceived by Tom Espiner; and the use of film core bobbins to create the sound of DEER's hooves, conceived by Ruth Sullivan. The bobbins come from the centre of film reels - a nod to the development of Foley as a moving image art form.

What follows is a list of Foley materials used in *Cow / Deer* - extensive but, as this text is being written prior to rehearsals, likely not exhaustive:

straw bale	bird callers	pair of socks
hay bale	dog whistle	coconut shells
turf strips	corrugated iron	sandpaper
bay tree	lollipop sticks	leather tag
fake willow tree	leather satchel	chamois leathers
ornamental grass pots	gardening gloves	towels
mint	white cotton glove	tea towel
pak choi	fake bunch of grapes	fake foliage
camouflage net	polystyrene balls	rope
bowls	leather belts	sofa cushions
tinsel	paintbrush	water bladder
raffia	fake fur	metal watering can
plastic bucket	mini mop	metal container

egg cups

handcream

hot water bottle

knee cushions

hairbrush

baton

dried cannellini beans

cornflour bag

key with ring

bobbins

rubber dampeners

tie

hessian

plaster of paris

potato chipper

wooden pallet

luggage weight spring

trolley

wooden drill

suitcases

bark mulch

fine and coarse gravel

pebbles

rocks

sand

Katie Mitchell, Nina Segal and Melanie Wilson

Cow | Deer

One

5.30 a.m.

Early August. England. Dawn.

A wooded area. Dusty. Dry. Red kite flies above.

A faint wind blows through the trees.

A rabbit leaves its burrow. Hears a rustle. Freezes. Sniffs the air.

A fox steps through the brambles – rabbit smells fox – skitters off. The fox follows – twigs snapping beneath its feet.

A squirrel hurries up a tree, then eats a nut.

A badger passes by, then disappears into its sett.

The squirrel scurries off, startled by the badger.

Small hooves approaching on compacted earth – it is a roe **Deer**, one year old, alone.

Deer pauses – listening – checks the environment is safe.

Deer feels an insect – she stamps her hoof to shake it off.

Deer notices ripe blackberries – moves to the bramble bush to nose for them.

A robin flies out of the brambles, startled.

Deer returns to eating – nibbling at blackberries, then tugging at a tree shoot.

A quad bike in the distance. **Deer** stops eating – listens. Thrumming of an engine. Wheels. **Deer** continues eating.

Sudden commotion, as a blackbird flies out of the tree.

Composition: a collage made from field recordings that rises and recedes, giving way to a woodland.

Field recording: nuthatches, robins, blue tits, great tits, chaffinches, diverse old woodland, oak trees above.

Field recording: a red kite calls above.

Foley: blue tinsel, magnetic tape.

Foley: bare hands, earth, fur, breath.

Foley: raffia, foliage, gloves, lollipop sticks, chamois.

Foley: foliage, belt, brush, lollipop sticks, bark.

Foley: foliage, forearms for weight, earth, mulch, badger breather, chamois, leather.

Foley: foliage, brush, scampering.

Foley: bobbins, raffia.

Sound design: the woodland shifts to **Deer**'s *perspective, and rotates around as* **Deer**'s *ears swivel, listening.*

Foley: small leather chamois.

Foley: fresh foliage.

Foley: leather, robin tweeter.

Foley: fresh foliage.

Sound design: distant quad bike.
Sound design: **Deer**'s *listening swivels to the quad bike sound.*

Field recording: blackbird warning cry.

The blackbird flies off, alarmed by Deer's presence.

Deer moves off – hooves stepping over soil, rocks, compacted earth.

Stillness.

Two

6 a.m.

A mixed arable dairy farm – the nursery cow field.

The sun is up now – air is warm and still – no breeze.

The sounds of agriculture – a tractor reversing, heavy wheels on concrete, as a dog barks in the distance.

A combine harvester two fields away – a steady hum of threshing – whirring – engines thrum.

A metal water trough sits at the edge of the cow field.

Sound of the quad bike, nearer – passing, then receding.

The sound of hooves on grass – a **Cow** appears.

She's two years old – thirsty and heavily pregnant.

She steps – slowly and heavily – through mud, towards the trough.

A horse-fly lands on **Cow**'s ear – bites – she flicks it off – scratches her head on the trough.

Cow leans her head and drinks – tongue into water – water into open mouth – swallow – repeat. Water drips from **Cow**'s head into the metal trough.

A fly buzzes around **Cow**'s ears – she flicks it off.

Foley: foliage, gloves.

Foley: earth, raffia, camouflage net, bark.

Composition: the collage of field recording rises under the woodland – then cuts.

Field recording: A nursery cow field on a dairy farm.

Sound design: tractor reversing in farmyard, dog barking mid-distance.

Sound design: combine harvester in the fields behind.

Sound design: steady sound of water trickling on left.

Sound design: quad bike passing by.
Foley: drill bit, watering can, spring.

Foley: on turf, coconut shells, packaging, socks.

Sound design: field recording shifts to **Cow**'s *perspective.*

Foley: wet tea towel on leather, plus chamois, in bowl.

Field recording: fly buzzes around **Cow**'s *left ear.*

Foley: watering can, leather, satchel.

Field recording: fly buzzes around **Cow**'s *left ear.*
Foley: little leather strap, satchel.

Cow leaves the trough – walks through the mud onto the grass – brushes over docks.

A car passes along the nearby road – a blast of music, then the car recedes.

Cow moves towards the herd – a dozen cows, all pregnant too – their bodies heavy, present – then continues on.

Cow steps through a cowpat.

A cloud of insects rise around her hooves – she flicks them off.

A swallow dives – hunting the scattered insects – wheels away.

Cow carries on – hooves brushing through lush grass.

Cow pauses – urinates – the liquid pools between her hooves.

She bends her head – tears off a mouthful of grass. **Cow** chews.

A passenger plane passes – sound of an engine far above. The plane recedes.

Three

6.05 a.m.

Woodland. A light breeze.

The same plane – louder now – directly over the woodland.

Deer steps through the trees – then pauses – listens to the plane.

A wood pigeon calls out – **Deer** pauses, listens, then continues on.

A car rumbles by on the road – again, **Deer** pauses – listening – faint sound of music from the car – it grows in volume – then recedes.

Deer moves on – stopping to nose among the vegetation.

Foley: wet tea towel on leather, plus chamois, in bowl, blue tinsel.

Sound design: car passes, music.

Field recording: **Cow** *passes the herd.*

Foley: toast and egg carton, chamois.

Sound design: insects rise on all sides.
Foley: tinsel, mini-mop, leather, towel snap.

Foley: bird whistle, baton, glove.

Foley: coconut hooves on turf.

Foley: water bladder, water trough.

Foley: turf rip, then cornflour bag chewing.

Sound design: plane overhead.

Field recording: woodland birds and breeze.

Sound design: plane directly above the woodland.
Sound shifts to **Deer**'s *perspective.*

Foley: bobbins, hay bale, foliage.

Field recording: wood pigeon.

Sound design: car passes away to left.
Foley: bobbin scrape on bark.

Foley: bobbins, foliage.

Layers of sound – wind turbines – a train, in the distance –
a red kite, wheeling overhead – dog barking, further off –
Deer's ears flick towards each sound – assessing for danger.

Deer shits – small pellets landing on the earth.

Deer moves on – deeper into the trees – moving into thick
canopy and undergrowth – searching for sustenance.

A light summer shower begins – raindrops patter on dry
ground, vegetation, leaves. The rain becomes heavy for a
moment – then lightens again. The summer shower stops.

Deer shakes the rain from her coat.

Deer leaves the woodland – walks into an open field – takes
a mouthful of long grass.

Deer urinates.

Deer sniffs the air, then moves on – cloven hooves over
damp ground.

Four

6.30 a.m.

The nursery cow field – after the rain.

Cow leans down to the grass – rips off a mouthful.

Cow chews.

Scrape of a metal gate in the middle distance – opened –
closed.

The sound of the herd moving – shifting – parting – as the
farmer steps into the field.

Cow stops chewing – listens – as the farmer moves towards
her, boots on grass.

Sound design: wind turbines, train, red kite and dog crowd closer for a moment from left, right, behind and above.

Foley: fake grapes on raffia on straw bale.

Foley: bobbins, bark, foliage.

Field recording: light rain begins.
Foley: leather, hands, raffia, bark, leaves, camouflage net.

Foley: satchel, leather, leather tag.

Foley: bobbins, earth, hay, fresh foliage.

Foley: water container with camouflage net, beaker of water, trickled through hands.

Foley: bobbins, earth, hay.

Field recording: nursery cow field.

Foley: fresh foliage, raffia, mint, tea leaves, turf, cornflour bag, wet tea towel.

Foley: cornflour bag.

Sound design: rusty metal gate opens (recording of foley gate, distanced).

Field recording: herd moving.
Foley: footsteps, turf.

Foley and sound design: turf square, footsteps (in booth).

The farmer's voice is faintly audible – female – checking, calming, counting – voice more of a rhythm or a texture, than verbal language.

The farmer reaches **Cow** – greets her – voice familiar and warm.

The farmer pats **Cow**'s body, walks around her.

The farmer scratches **Cow**'s side.

Cow chews, as the farmer walks back to the gate.

Clang of the metal gate, as the farmer leaves the field.

An insect buzzes – landing on **Cow**'s ear.

Cow flicks it off – it flies away.

Cow steps towards the hedgerow, a thick mess of hawthorn, blackthorn, hazel. In the hedgerow's centre is a wire fence.

A sparrow calls out from the hedgerow, as **Cow** approaches.

Cow dips her head to the hedgerow, searching out a willow leaf.

She sniffs.

Cow eats.

A harvest mouse is disturbed by **Cow**.

The mouse scurries off, away from **Cow**, moving deeper into the hedgerow, stopping and starting as she runs.

The mouse meets a second mouse – they greet each other with a squeak, then move in separate directions – each mouse scurrying off through the undergrowth.

Foley and sound design: farmer counting, greeting cows (unintelligible).

Foley and sound design: farmer greets **Cow** *(unintelligible).*

Field recording: **Cow** *breathes out.*
Foley: footsteps, hand on body.
Sound design: farmer's footsteps walk around **Cow**.

Foley: clothing.

Foley: leather satchel with cornflour bag.
Sound design: footsteps retreat away (in booth).

Sound design: metal gate closes.

Field recording: fly buzzes around **Cow**'s *ears.*
Foley: leather tag, glove.

Foley: mini-mop, leather, raffia.

Foley: coconut shells, turf.
Field recording: sparrows chatter in busy hedgerow ecosystem.

Field recording: sparrow warning.

Foley: fake foliage.

Field recording: **Cow** *sniffs.*

Foley: mint, fake foliage, gardening gloves.

Foley: mouse squeak.

Foley: lollipop sticks, raffia, foliage additions.
Field recording: internal hedgerow ecosystem.
Sound design: sound shifts to the mouse's perspective.

Foley: mouse squeak.
Foley: fingertips.
Sound design: sound shifts to second mouse's perspective.

The second mouse freezes – tense, vigilant – as **Deer**'s nose – inquisitive – sniffs in the hedgerow, up ahead. The mouse turns and runs away – small footsteps recede into the hedgerow.

Five

6.45 a.m.

The hedgerow – from the other side of it.

Deer noses in the hedgerow – then moves off across the field, moving towards the woodland.

Deer enters the woodland – small hooves placed carefully between the roots and stones – moving into the trees.

A twig snaps – **Deer** freezes – turns her head and hooves towards the sound.

The sound of something small and scurrying – a squirrel scampers up a trunk – **Deer** pauses – listening.

The squirrel scampers off – **Deer** carries on.

A stream, ahead of **Deer** – she hears the moving water – steps towards it – faster now.

Deer reaches the stream – steps into the water – bends her neck down to the stream to drink – remaining vigilant.

A dipper calls out – **Deer** stops drinking – lifts her head.

The dipper lands on a branch and calls again.

The dipper briefly dives under the water – searching, hunting – then emerges with an insect in its beak.

The dipper flaps away – shaking the water from its wings.

Deer steps into the stream – plunges her head under the water.

Deer lifts her head out of the water – shaking the water off.

Field recording: **Deer** *sniff.*
Foley: mouse squeak, fingertips, raffia.
Field recording: external hedgerow.

Field recording: hedgerow in front, field behind.

Foley: bobbins, foliage, twigs, hay bale.
Field recording: woodland.

Foley: bobbins, earth, bark, stones.

Foley: lasagne sheets, bobbins, earth.

Foley: foliage, bark, leather belt, brush.

Foley: foliage, bark.

Foley: bobbins, stones, foliage.
Field recording: woodland stream.

Foley: bobbins, gravel, bigger pebbles.

Foley: bird whistle.

Foley: bird whistle, foliage.

Foley: foliage, water tank, leather glove.

Foley: leather glove, water drops.

Foley: gravel, bobbins, pebbles.
Field recording: underwater soundscape.

Foley: leather, satchel, water drops.

A nuthatch calls out – flies in – lands upon a bush. **Deer** watches as the bird moves lightly, searching in the bush.

The nuthatch finds a clump of berries – shiny, perfect – hidden in the leaves. It takes a berry in its mouth – another – eating quickly – as **Deer** watches it.

Deer sniffs the air – nose twitching – licks her lips.

Deer steps through the water – crosses the stream – and scrambles up the other side – climbing the rocky bank.

The nuthatch calls out – flutters off – alarmed.

Deer steps towards the bush – she noses through the leaves, then finds a berry – takes it in her teeth – she pulls – a twig snaps – **Deer** chews – swallows – finds another berry – eats.

An insect lands on **Deer** – she flicks her ear to shake it off.

Six

10 a.m.

The nursery cow field.

Cow's standing by the hedgerow – there's a fence within it and a footpath on the other side.

Cow tears a strand of grass – she chews.

A new sound, in the distance – a dog whistle.

Cow stops eating – looks toward the sound.

A small dog is approaching fast – it squeezes underneath the fence and through the hedgerow – closing in on **Cow**.

The dog nears **Cow** – barking – circling her.

Foley: foliage, bird caller.

Foley: fake grapes, bark, stick, foliage.

Foley: mouth sound.
Field recording: **Deer** *sniff.*

Foley: water tank, bobbins, pebbles, gravel.

Foley: bird whistle pouch, foliage, leather glove.

Foley: pulling foliage, cornflour bag, mouth eating.

Field recording: insect.
Foley: brown glove sideways.

Field recording: nursery cow field.

Sound design: sound shifts to **Cow**'s *perspective.*

Foley: mint, cornflour bag, coconut hooves, turf.

Sound design: dog whistle.

Foley: leather bag, coconut shells.

Foley and sound design: fingertips, key (in booth).

Sound design: dog paws move back and forth in 180-degree arc in front of **Cow**.
Field recording: dog barking.

Cow turns – trying to face the dog head-on. She snorts.

The dog's owners – beyond the hedgerow – try to call the dog.

The dog encircles **Cow** – leaping towards her – biting at her ankles. **Cow** stamps her feet on grass and dirt.

A whistle – the dog heeds the call – turns back to the hedgerow – lopes away – back underneath the fence – back to its owners.

Cow shits. The shit falls – heavy, warm – onto the grass.

A car passes on the road – a can thrown from its window.

The wind picks up – a plastic bag flaps on a fence – the weather's changing – growing cooler now.

Cow moves across the field – passes the other cows, their bodies heavy, moving, chewing, shitting – until she is alone.

Cow shifts her weight – swishing her tail from side-to-side.

She paces in a circle – and then bellows.

Something's changing – something's drawing near.

Cow's amniotic sac emerges from her hindquarters.

Birth is approaching.

Seven

10.15 a.m.

Woodland.

Deer at the berry bush, still – eating – listening.

She hears wind in the trees – and, further off, **Cow** bellowing.

Foley: coconut shells, turf.
Field recording: **Cow** *snort.*

Sound design: dog whistle, shouts from a distance (unintelligible).

Foley: fingertips, key.
Foley: coconut shells, turf.
Field recording: dog barking.

Sound design: dog whistle.
Foley: fingertips, key.

Foley: blue catering roll, damp, in hands onto bale.

Sound design: passing car.
Foley: can, on concrete slab.

Field recording: wind picks up.
Foley: plastic bag.

Field recording: herd moving across field.
Foley: coconut shells, turf.

Foley: mini-mop, rope.

Field recording: **Cow** *bellows.*

Foley: liquid soap between hands.

Field recording: woodland stream, birdsong.

Foley: bobbins, foliage, raffia.

Foley: tinsel.
Sound design: **Cow** *bellowing.*

A military jet passes – low, loud, violent – overhead.

Deer moves off – hooves stepping fast on forest floor.

She hears a new sound through the trees – the sound of children – laughing – playing – **Deer** stops running – pausing – listening.

The children's voices grow closer – they shriek, seeing **Deer**.

Deer turns and runs – the children chase her, but their shouts grow distant as **Deer** easily outpaces them.

Deer runs back through the woodland – hooves on dirt – on pebbles – back across the stream – small rocks disturbed – twigs snap beneath her feet – running fast – then:

A buzz – electric – stops her in her tracks – it's an electric fence.

Deer listens – hesitant – takes two steps back – hooves on dirt.

Deer sniffs – smell of cow dung, exhaust – listens – sounds of agriculture – tractor, barking dog, clang of a metal gate.

Another sound – **Cow** bellowing – much closer now.

Deer is at the cow field – **Cow** stood, just beyond the fence.

A moment – the two creatures, **Cow** and **Deer**, facing each other – then **Deer** turns – runs, fast – back into the trees.

Eight

10.30 a.m.

The cow nursery field.

Cow is in labour now – she bellows – low.

She shifts her body – slowly lowers herself to the ground.

Her breath is heavy – audible – she snorts – inhales – bellows.

Sound design: military jet passing.

Foley: bobbins, earth, bark.

Sound design: children laughing, shouting (unintelligible).

Sound design: children shriek (unintelligible), then shush each other.

Foley: bobbins, earth, foliage, bark.
Sound design: shouts (unintelligible).

Foley: bobbins, raffia, foliage, bark, earth.

Sound design: electric fence.
Foley: bobbins, earth.

Foley: bobbins, earth.

Field recording: **Deer** *sniffs.*
Sound design: tractor, dog barks, clang of a metal gate.

Field recording: **Cow** *bellowing.*

Foley: bobbins, hay bale, bark.

Field recording: cow nursery field.

Field recording: **Cow** *bellowing.*

Foley: coconuts, forearms, cushion, turf, shoulder.
Field recording: **Cow** *bellowing.*

Field recording: **Cow** *bellow, breath, strain.*

The rain begins again – just lightly – sky gone clouded – grey.

The sound of birdsong – insects – wind in leaves.

Cow bellows – low, loud, forceful – draws breath – bellows again.

The calf is coming – hooves protruding now from **Cow**'s vagina – still contained within the amniotic sac.

Cow labours – straining, pushing – bellows – body working hard.

Cow bellows – labours – calf is almost here.

Nine

10.35 a.m.

Woodland.

Deer moves fast – hooves on forest floor – through vegetation.

Cow's bellows echo through the trees – far off, yet audible.

Deer pauses – listens – turns towards the sound – pausing a moment – then continues on.

The ground beneath **Deer**'s feet changes – from forest floor to dirt to tarmac – then a new sound – unfamiliar – a road.

Cow bellows, in the distance – **Deer**, again, turns towards the sound.

A sudden roar – a car – loud, thunderous – approaches, bearing down on **Deer**.

Deer freezes, for a moment – then reacts – fast hooves on tarmac – as the car grows close – closer – then passes her.

The car recedes – drives off into the distance – **Deer** crosses the road, hooves over tarmac – reaching the safety of the other side.

Field recording: light rain.

Field recording: birdsong, insects, wind.

Field recording: **Cow** *bellow, breath, longer bellow.*

Foley: hand cream between hands.

Foley: hand cream, coconut shells, turf, rope.
Field recording: **Cow** *bellow, breath, strain.*

Foley: hand cream, pak choi, water.
Field recording: **Cow** *bellow.*

Sound design: woodland in motion.

Foley: bobbins, bark, earth, foliage.

Sound design: **Cow** *bellow receding.*

Foley: bobbins, earth, raffia.
Sound design: woodland stills.

Foley: bobbins, concrete and gravel slab.

Sound design: **Cow** *bellow, far off.*

Sound design: car very close and loud.

Foley: bobbins, concrete and gravel slab.
Sound design: car close then passes by.

Sound design: car recedes.
Foley: gravel, raffia, turf.

A cornfield – divided by a hedgerow from the road – there's a gap in the hedgerow – **Deer** runs through.

The sound of the road recedes – as **Deer** walks – slowly, calmer now – into the stalks of corn – as they envelop her.

Far off, now – faint, yet audible – **Cow** bellows, labouring.

Ten

12 p.m.

The nursery cow field.

Cow in the height of labour now – she bellows, loud and long.

Her breath is strained – her body working hard now – labouring.

Birdsong, in momentary quiet.

The calf's snout and hooves protruding from **Cow** now.

Cow bellows – bellows – breathes.

A new sound – shrill – a siren – somewhere far away.

Cow bellows – breathes – bellows – bellows – breathes.

Car in the distance – sound grows louder – then recedes.

Cow bellows – bearing down – the sound of wet and flesh and fluid – straining – rupturing – the amniotic sac bursts open – liquid spilling – as the calf's head emerges from the **Cow**'s vagina.

Cow bellows as calf's body follows – sliding wetly out.

The calf drops to the floor.

Cow leans to lick the calf – her rough tongue on its side.

Cow breathes on calf – nudging it with her head – then licks.

Calf gasps – then starts to breathe.

Foley: turf, earth.

Field recording: crickets, swifts.
Foley: foliage, long grass, earth.

Sound design: **Cow** *bellows.*

Field recording: nursery cow field.

Field recording: **Cow** *bellows.*

Field recording: **Cow** *deep breath.*

Field recording: nursery cow field, birdsong.

Foley: hand cream, pak choi.

Field recording: **Cow** *bellows twice, breathes.*

Sound design: police siren.

Field recording: **Cow** *bellows, breathes.*

Sound design: car passes and recedes.

Field recording: **Cow** *bellows.*
Foley: pak choi, cream, balloon burst.

Foley: pak choi, cream, balloon burst, melon flesh.
Field recording: **Cow** *bellows.*

Foley: melon half turned, bladder, liquid, wet towel.

Foley: sandpaper, cream, gardening glove, wet towel.

Field recording: **Cow** *breathes and nudges.*
Foley: sandpaper, cream, gardening glove, wet towel.

Field recording: calf gasps and breathes.

Cow keeps licking her calf – licking her body, nudging her.

Calf shifts its body – tries to stand – falls – tries again – up on its feet now – wobbling but upright – takes a step – tottering.

Calf stands and falls four times – **Cow** noses at it – nudges it towards her body – calf suckles **Cow**.

A siren – once more – in the distance – far away.

Eleven

5 p.m.

The cornfield.

The wind moves through the corn, as birds wheel overhead.

It's later now – the sky is darkened slightly – air grown cool.

A field mouse scurries through the stalks.

A corn bunting pecks across the ground.

Small insects – ants and spiders – bustle through the stalks.

An insect flits across the sky – a swallow dives after it, hunting.

Through all of this, **Deer** sleeps – nestled among the stalks – her ear flaps slightly, as she snores – safe, hidden in the corn.

Listening.

A new sound – heavy and mechanical – rhythmic – unceasing – drawing near – a combine harvester. The combine harvester is at the top edge of the field – the point **Deer** entered from. There is no other means to leave the field.

The combine harvester moves slowly – working from the outside of the field towards the centre – in ever-decreasing circuits.

Foley: green glove, wet towel, against grain.
Field recording: **Cow** *breathes and nudges.*

Foley: taped egg cups on turf, wet and dry towel mix.

Field recording: **Cow** *licking, breathing, grunting.*
Foley: bobbins, leather, wet towel.

Sound design: siren.

Field recording: swallows call and wheel.

Field recording: breeze in corn stalks and distant canopy.

Foley: foliage, corn field shimmer, slight wind.

Foley: raffia, fingertips.

Foley: raffia, fingertips.

Foley: raffia, long grass.

Foley: insect, baton.
Field recording: swallow screech.

Field recording: **Deer** *snores.*

Sound design: a combine harvester enters the field, in the top left corner.

Sound design: combine harvester slowly makes its way down the left side of the field, still far off.

The harvest mice react – begin to move through **Deer**'s sleeping place, with rising panic.

Deer jolts awake – aware of threat – she stands and sniffs.

The combine harvester rumbles behind **Deer** – humming – threshing – whirring – shaking the ground as it passes by.

The smaller animals are streaming past **Deer** now – their bodies turning, twisting, through the stalks of corn.

The combine harvester continues – moving in slow circuits, drawing closer to **Deer** and the smaller animals – before receding – then approaching once again on **Deer**'s right side.

The smaller animals are panicking – escaping – trying to.

The combine harvester kicks up a storm of dust and stalks – again receding, before approaching a third time – drawing closer still.

Foley: raffia, grass.

Foley: bobbins, earth, hay.
Field recording: **Deer** *sniffs.*

Sound design: combine harvester passes behind **Deer**, *closer now.*
Foley: trolley, suitcase, drill bit rattled.
+
Foley: metal bucket, dried beans.
+
Foley: leather wing flaps on straw.
+
Foley: beans dropped onto straw and camouflage net and fake foliage.
+
Foley: chipper with beans.

Foley: tinsel, straw, polystyrene balls.

Sound design: combine passes on **Deer***'s right side, closer.*
Foley: trolley, suitcase, drill bit rattled.
+
Foley: tinsel, straw, polystyrene balls, lollipop sticks snapping.
+
Foley: metal bucket, dried beans.
+
Foley: leather wing flaps on straw.
+
Foley: beans dropped onto straw and camouflage net and fake foliage.
+
Foley: chipper with beans.

Foley: tinsel, straw, polystyrene balls.

Sound design: the combine approaches from the front and very close.
Foley: trolley, suitcase, drill bit rattled.
+

The other animals are scattering – making a break for it – the displaced mice and insects racing through the corn.

The uncut area of corn in which **Deer** shelters narrows – she stands – stamps – moves in circles – agitated now.

Deer runs – fast – terrified – made clumsy now with fear – breaking her cover – crossing the corn stubble – the combine harvester receding – **Deer** crosses the field – then:

Deer's at the road – her hooves on tarmac – scared and skittering – a car roars past – **Deer** freezes – hesitates – tries to turn back – she is afraid – disorientated – then:

A second car approaches – brakes hard – but it's too late –

Deer is hit – knocked over by the car – thrown violently to the side of the road – crumpled – bleeding heavily.

The car continues – sound receding as it drives away.

Twelve

5.10 p.m.

The nursery cow field.

Cow and calf together – dozing – both exhausted from the birth.

A dog barks in the distance – the other cows shift restlessly.

Calf stirs – **Cow** leans to lick her – soft – maternal and instinctive.

Sound of a distant quad bike – it approaches, pulling a trailer.

Foley: tinsel, straw, polystyrene balls.
+
Foley: metal bucket, dried beans.
+
Foley: leather wing flaps on straw.
+
Foley: beans dropped onto straw and camouflage net and fake foliage.
+
Foley: chipper with beans, pak choi breaks.

Foley: bobbins, earth, hay.

Foley: bobbins, raffia, earth.
Sound design: combine harvester recedes.

Foley: bobbins, gravel, concrete slab.
Sound design: car passes **Deer**.

Sound design: car braking.

Sound design: impact and crunch of body on metal.
Foley: metal, bobbins, cushion, gravel.

Sound design: car recedes.
Foley: **Deer** *breath.*

Field recording: nursery cow field.

Field recording: small vocalisations from **Cow** *and calf.*

Sound design: dog bark, herd shifts.

Foley: hand cream, leather, fake fur.

Sound design: quad bike in distance.

The metal gate to the field clangs open – then shut.

The quad bike – with trailer – approaches **Cow** and calf.

Cow stands – protective – as calf stirs between her feet.

The quad bike engine dies – the farmer dismounts and approaches – heavy boots on grass.

Cow snorts a warning, as the farmer reaches for the calf.

The farmer murmurs – shushing – comforting – and reaches out a hand to stroke the calf.

Cow exhales heavily, unsure – becoming agitated – then:

The farmer lifts the calf – grunting slightly from the exertion – swings it up into the quad bike trailer.

Cow paces – following her calf.

Cow bellows – calf calls out, confused – some movement in the herd – they shift – aware – unsure.

The farmer climbs onto the quad bike – starts the engine – driving back towards the nursery gate.

Cow bellows, following the quad bike – calf calls back.

The engine slows – the quad bike stops – the metal gate clangs open and the quad bike revs again – then roars out of the field.

The gate clangs shut – the quad bike drives into the farmyard.

Cow stands at the fence – it buzzes with electric charge.

Calf is heard – calling – growing fainter – further away.

Cow bellows – calling to her calf.

Sound design: metal gate open and closed.

Sound design: quad bike approaches.

Foley: coconut shells, turf, cushion.
Field recording: small vocalisations from **Cow** *and calf.*

Sound design: quad bike engine stops.
Foley: turf square, footsteps (in booth).

Field recording: **Cow** *snorts.*

Foley: farmer murmurs (unintelligible).
Foley: hand on body, fake fur.

Sound design: **Cow** *breath.*

Foley: farmer grunts.
Foley: cushion, leather, metal, hay.

Foley: coconut shells, turf, satchel, rope.

Field recording: **Cow** *bellows.*
Field recording: calf calls back.
Field recording: movement in the herd.

Sound design: quad bike.
Foley: footsteps, turf, fabric.

Field recording: **Cow** *bellows.*
Field recording: calf calls back.
Sound design: quad bike.
Foley: coconut shells, turf, rope, satchel.

Sound design: quad bike slows, stops, idles, starts and drives.
Foley: drill bit, spring, metal sheet.

Sound design: quad bike recedes.
Foley: drill bit, spring, metal sheet.

Field recording: electric fence to left and water trough.

Field recording: calf calls, fainter.

Field recording: **Cow** *bellows.*

The calf calls out for **Cow**.

Cow bellows back.

The calf calls out for **Cow**.

Cow bellows back.

The calf calls out for **Cow**.

Cow bellows back.

The calf is no longer audible – but still, **Cow** bellows back.

Cow bellows.

Cow bellows.

Cow bellows.

Cow bellows.

Thirteen

5.20 p.m.

The road.

Deer lays, bleeding, by the road – her breathing ragged – legs twitching with pain. **Deer** tries to move – she can't. She lays there, at the roadside, as the world continues on.

Above her, a small aircraft passes – unheeding and unaware.

A red kite wheels in the sky above **Deer**'s head.

Birds call to one another – hidden in the trees.

A car approaches – sound of brakes – the car slows – pulls in – stops – the door opens – a man in office shoes steps out.

Footsteps approach – **Deer** tries to move – she can't – she waits – tense – terrified – as the footsteps draw close.

Thunder rumbles in the distance – rain begins to fall.

Field recording: calf calls, fainter.

Field recording: **Cow** *bellows.*

Field recording: calf calls, fainter.

Field recording: **Cow** *bellows.*

Field recording: calf calls, fainter.

Field recording: **Cow** *bellows.*

Field recording: **Cow** *bellows.*

Field recording: **Cow** *bellows.*

Field recording: **Cow** *bellows.*

Field recording: **Cow** *bellows.*

Field recording: **Cow** *bellows.*

Sound design: shift into **Deer**'s *perspective.*
Field recording: hedgerow by the road.

Field recording: **Deer**'s *breath, laboured.*
Foley: bobbins, gravel.

Sound design: small leisure aircraft passes above.

Sound design: a red kite wheels across the sky, calling.

Field recording: birds chatter in hedgerow.

Sound design: car approaches, brakes, stops, door opens.
Foley: footsteps, gravel, concrete slab.

Foley: footsteps, gravel, concrete slab.
Foley: bobbins, gravel.

Sound design: thunder, rain.

A quad bike passes – slows – then picks up speed again – recedes.

The man's footsteps reach **Deer** – he inhales sharply – shocked – kneels down beside her – leans in close.

Deer scrabbles in the dirt – she tries to stand – she can't.

A hand reaches towards her – slow – fingers against her side – **Deer** flinches – tries to stand again – she can't – she struggles – wild – frightened – bleeding – the man pulls his hand away – he is afraid – of her – the blood – his helplessness –

He straightens – stepping backwards – stumbles slightly – turns and walks away – quickly – to the safety of his car.

The man pauses – hand on handle – turns to look at **Deer**.

The rain is heavy now – as **Deer** lays, twitching, in the road.

The man pulls the door open – climbs inside – closes the door – puts on his seatbelt – engine on – the radio starts playing – pop music – he puts the car in gear and drives away.

Deer lays – still breathing, bleeding – on the road. Her breath is fainter now – rattling – gasping – thin.

Around her are the sounds of birdsong – cars passing – plane overhead – leaves rustle faintly in the wind.

We listen for a long, long time – and then:

The quad bike returns – drives up to **Deer** – then brakes. The engine is turned off – the farmer dismounts and approaches **Deer** – stands over her.

The farmer exhales – lifts the gun she carries – takes the safety catch off – cocks the triggers – pauses – and then:

Shoots.

Sound design: quad bike passes.

Foley: footsteps, gravel, concrete slab, breath.

Foley: bobbins, gravel, cushion.
Foley: fake fur, bobbins, gravel.
Foley: intake of man's breath.

Foley: footsteps, gravel, concrete slab.

Sound design: car door handle.

Field recording: rain.

Sound design: car door opens, closes, seatbelt, engine starts, radio, drives away.
Foley: footsteps, gravel, fabric.

Sound design: **Deer** *breath.*

Field recording: birdsong, red kite calls overhead.
Foley: tinsel.
Sound design: plane overhead.

Foley: boots, gravel, concrete (in booth), metal.
Sound design: quad bike approaches.

Foley: farmer exhales.
Sound design: gun handling, safety catch, trigger.

Sound design: shot sound cuts almost immediately to silence after triggering. This ends the **Deer**'s *perspective. After the silence, the sound of the road and hedgerow fades back in.*

The gunshot draws the birds out of the trees – they screech and flap and wheel – then settle – quiet once again – as life goes on.

Fourteen

5.30 p.m.

Woodland. Early August. Early evening.

The sound of wind – of passing cars – birdsong – a rabbit, moving softly – insects flitting between trees – birds wheeling overhead.

The sky is growing darker – wind rising, thunder drawing close.

Shift to:

The road.

A car passes – another car – another rumbles past.

A plane flies over – many miles above the ground.

A red kite drifts through the dusk – watching – looking down.

Shift to:

The nursery cow field.

Cow stamps her feet – presses her body to the fence.

She bellows for her calf.

A train passes in the distance, sounds its horn.

Cow bellows for her calf.

A plastic bag flaps in the wind.

Cow bellows for her calf.

Cow bellows for her calf.

The sound of birdsong rises – then dies away.

Foley: leather gloves, foliage.
Field recording: bird warning calls.
Field recording: road and hedgerow returns to calm.

Field recording: woodland, insects, birdsong.

Sound design: car in distance.
Foley: foliage, raffia.

Foley: tinsel.

Field recording: hedgerow by the road.

Sound design: car passes, then another.

Sound design: plane overhead.

Sound design: red kite overhead.

Field recording: nursery cow field, electric fence, water trough, flies.

Foley: coconut shells, metal, earth.

Field recording: **Cow** *bellows.*

Sound design: train in distance.

Field recording: **Cow** *bellows.*

Foley: plastic bag.

Field recording: **Cow** *bellows.*

Field recording: **Cow** *bellows.*

Field recording: the cow field and birdsong die away.

Methuen Drama Contemporary Dramatists

include

John Arden (two volumes)
Arden & D'Arcy
Peter Barnes (three volumes)
Sebastian Barry
Mike Bartlett
Clare Barron
Brad Birch
Dermot Bolger
Edward Bond (ten volumes)
Howard Brenton (two volumes)
Leo Butler (two volumes)
Richard Cameron
Jim Cartwright
Caryl Churchill (two volumes)
Complicite
Sarah Daniels (two volumes)
Nick Darke
David Edgar (three volumes)
David Eldridge (two volumes)
Ben Elton
Per Olov Enquist
Dario Fo (two volumes)
Michael Frayn (four volumes)
John Godber (four volumes)
Paul Godfrey
James Graham (two volumes)
David Greig
John Guare
Lee Hall (two volumes)
Katori Hall
Peter Handke
Jonathan Harvey (two volumes)
Iain Heggie
Israel Horovitz
Declan Hughes
Terry Johnson (three volumes)
Sarah Kane
Barrie Keeffe
Bernard-Marie Koltès (two volumes)
Franz Xaver Kroetz
Kwame Kwei-Armah
David Lan
Bryony Lavery
Deborah Levy
Doug Lucie

Alistair MacDowall
Sabrina Mahfouz
David Mamet (six volumes)
Patrick Marber
Martin McDonagh
Duncan McLean
David Mercer (two volumes)
Anthony Minghella (two volumes)
Rory Mullarkey
Tom Murphy (six volumes)
Phyllis Nagy
Anthony Neilson (three volumes)
Peter Nichol (two volumes)
Philip Osment
Gary Owen
Louise Page
Stewart Parker (two volumes)
Joe Penhall (two volumes)
Stephen Poliakoff (three volumes)
David Rabe (two volumes)
Mark Ravenhill (three volumes)
Christina Reid
Philip Ridley (two volumes)
Willy Russell
Eric-Emmanuel Schmitt
Ntozake Shange
Sam Shepard (two volumes)
Martin Sherman (two volumes)
Christopher Shinn (two volumes)
Joshua Sobel
Wole Soyinka (two volumes)
Simon Stephens (five volumes)
Shelagh Stephenson
David Storey (three volumes)
C. P. Taylor
Sue Townsend
Judy Upton (two volumes)
Michel Vinaver (two volumes)
Arnold Wesker (two volumes)
Peter Whelan
Michael Wilcox
Roy Williams (four volumes)
David Williamson
Snoo Wilson (two volumes)
David Wood (two volumes)
Victoria Wood

Methuen Drama Modern Plays

include

Bola Agbaje
Ayad Akhtar
Edward Albee
Jean Anouilh
John Arden
Peter Barnes
Clare Barron
Sebastian Barry
Alistair Beaton
Brendan Behan
Edward Bond
William Boyd
Bertolt Brecht
Howard Brenton
Amelia Bullmore
Anthony Burgess
Leo Butler
Jim Cartwright
Lolita Chakrabarti
Caryl Churchill
Lucinda Coxon
Tim Crouch
Shelagh Delaney
Ishy Din
Claire Dowie
David Edgar
David Eldridge
Dario Fo
Michael Frayn
John Godber
James Graham
David Greig
John Guare
Lauren Gunderson
Peter Handke
David Harrower
Jonathan Harvey
Robert Holman
David Ireland
Sarah Kane

Barrie Keeffe
Jasmine Lee-Jones
Anders Lustgarten
Duncan Macmillan
David Mamet
Patrick Marber
Martin McDonagh
Alistair McDowall
Arthur Miller
Tom Murphy
Phyllis Nagy
Anthony Neilson
Peter Nichols
Ben Okri
Joe Orton
Vinay Patel
Joe Penhall
Luigi Pirandello
Stephen Poliakoff
Lucy Prebble
Peter Quilter
Mark Ravenhill
Philip Ridley
Willy Russell
Sam Shepard
Martin Sherman
Chris Shinn
Jackie Sibblies Drury
Wole Soyinka
Simon Stephens
Kae Tempest
Laura Wade
Anne Washburn
Timberlake Wertenbaker
Roy Williams
Snoo Wilson
Theatre Workshop
Frances Ya-Chu Cowhig
Benjamin Zephaniah

For a complete listing of
Methuen Drama titles, visit:
www.bloomsbury.com/drama

Follow us on X and keep up to date with
our news and publications
@MethuenDrama